I0493810

ISBN 978 - 0 - 9565802 - 3 - 8

Special thanks go to the students and tutors of the Summer Studio held at
the Cyprus College of Art in Larnaca, Cyprus, June 2007; and those of the
Kunst Leben, held in Irsee, Germany, July 2007, for their discussion with us
of some of these ideas.

Published in England (EU) by the Orage Press
16a Heaton Road, Mitcham, Surrey, CR4 2BU, England

© 2013 Copyright Clive Head and Michael Paraskos, all rights reserved

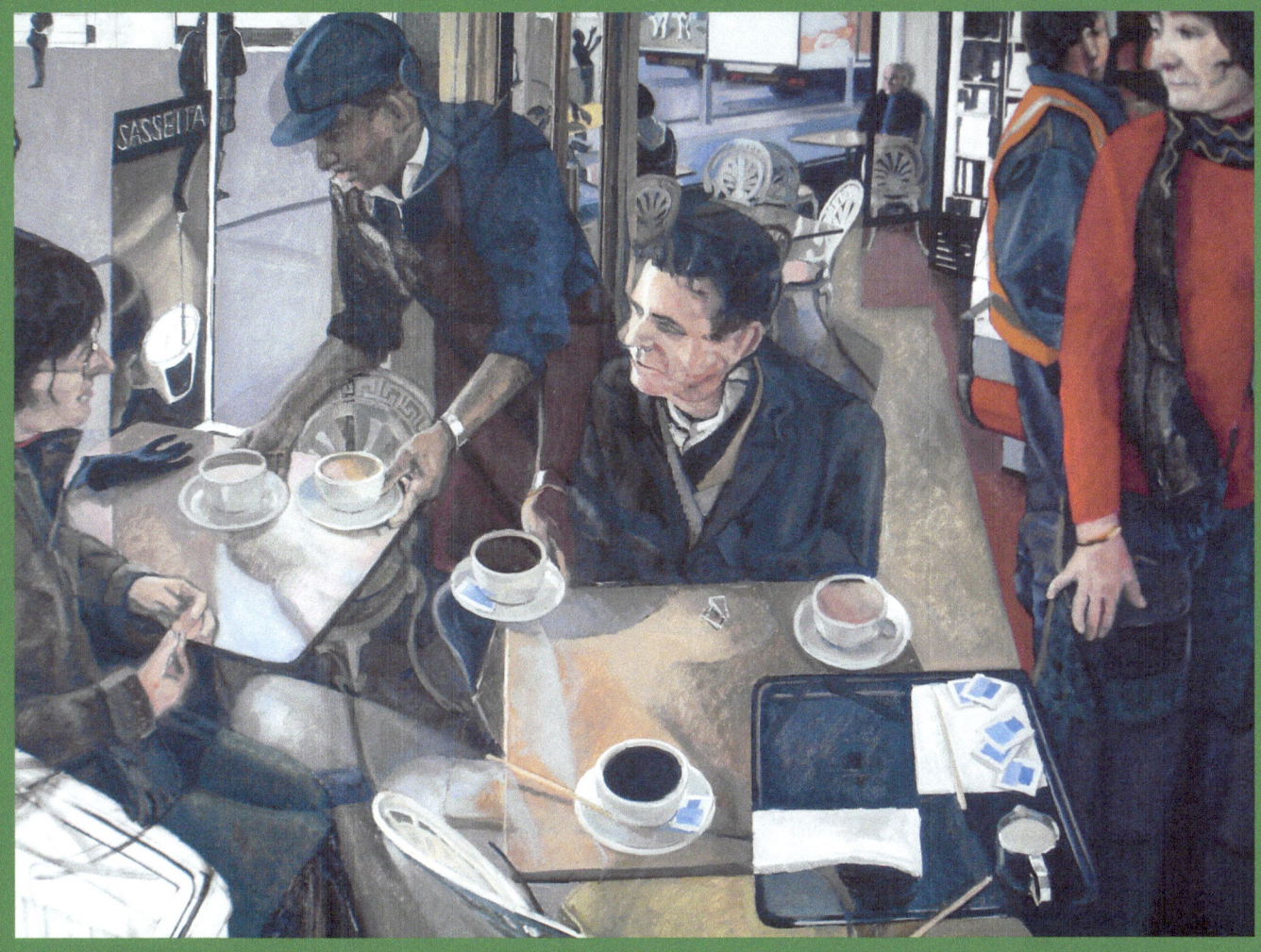

Clive Head's images appear courtesy of Marlborough Fine Art, London
© Clive Head 2013 All rights reserved

The New Aesthetics: An Introduction
By Michael Paraskos

Psychologists tell of a condition called Stockholm Syndrome in which a victim of abuse will identify so much with the abuser he comes to believe the abuse is justified. We could argue that art suffers from Stockholm Syndrome. After a century of abuse at the hands of Marcel Duchamp and his heirs many of the anti-art principles that underpin conceptualism are, paradoxically, accepted by artists who claim to oppose and even despise conceptual art.

Take the idea that art is about something. The phrase 'my art is about' is a common one, but by saying it we turn art into a form of concept illustration. When we say my art is about my feelings, or my memories, or a political or social event, what we really mean is here is my idea and here is my illustration of it. In that there is no difference with basic conceptualism.

This suggests there is a serious problem in pitting oneself against conceptual art, not because a lot of artists and art lovers do not who share a dislike of conceptualism, but because many of them are unwittingly corrupted by conceptualist thinking. If we dislike conceptualist art because it illustrates pre-existing ideas we inevitably dislike a lot of apparently non-conceptualist art because it too illustrates pre-existing ideas.

This is particularly apparent in photorealism, where very few practitioners consider themselves conceptualists. But copying a photograph, or even a manipulated digital image, is by its nature a conceptualist act, a repetition of a pre-existing idea, even if we use paint. Indeed, European painters such as Gerhard Richter have built a career on exploring this conceptualist aspect of photorealism.

Faced with this the logical position for anyone wanting to propose artistic values that are not conceptualist is to become a kind of nihilist, rejecting the art world completely. Out of that rejection a new set of possibilities has space to emerge. This is what motivated the British artist Clive Head and myself in 2007 when we found ourselves in the somewhat comic position of trying to teach art at a summer camp in southern Germany to a group of students who spoke no English while we had no German. Forced back on ourselves, our conversations coalesced into a series of pithy sayings on the nature of art, later published as *The Aphorisms of Irsee*. In these we sought to summarise a set of basic principles on art, whilst also cracking a few jokes. In both cases this was an anti-conceptualist act, setting out an alternate basis for art, while also undermining through humour the po-faced tedium of so much conceptualist writing.

Yet what is important about the *Aphorisms* is not that it opposed conceptualism, it is the emphasis on setting a positive agenda for art irrespective of conceptualism. We came to call this agenda the New Aesthetics. As it developed we returned to the origin of the word aesthetics, which in its ancient Greek form was *aisthesis.* Unlike the modern word, *aisthesis* did not mean beauty or prettiness, it meant the act of experiencing the world through the physical senses. The ancient Greeks themselves contrasted this with conceptualism, or rather *mathesis,* which meant conceptualising an idea of the world in the mind.

An aesthetics based on *aisthesis* seems to fit far more fully the artistic process than conceptualist theory, or even historic aesthetic theory, as it focuses attention on material and physical things. This starts with the artist experiencing the physical world around them and this provoking a desire or need to respond. For artists that response is highly physical in the act of painting, for example, but it is also highly material in the artist's engagement with colour, brushes, canvas, linseed oil and turpentine. Each of these assaults a different sense and requires a unique physical response. It is also physical and material in the final outcome of the process, the painting, sculpture or other work that is produced.

All of this should seem obvious to an artist, but contrast it to the desensitised and dematerialised work of the average conceptualist. Also compare it to the notion of having an idea and illustrating it. An artist in this New Aesthetics scenario might have an initial impulse to make something because of an idea, or a feeling, or event, but the unpredictable nature of the aesthetic process, and the constant engagement with the material stuff of art, means that initial impulse is at best highly modified and possibly left far behind. In truth we can no longer say a work of art is about something, and instead have to acknowledge it is the product of an unpredictable development or process.

The evolution of the New Aesthetics is ongoing too, attracting the interest of others, most notably Alan Pocaro, an art educator in Chicago, and Pierluigi Sacco, a well known writer on art in Italy. It has also led to some surprising revelations about art. One of these we are working through now is the idea found in Greek Orthodox Christianity that by placing such an emphasis on physical and sensory experience we do not end up with a highly materialist art. Instead, again as in Orthodox Christian art, we seem to discover or create a material object that is both part of this world and transcendent or other worldly. This has come to underpin how Clive sees his paintings, and is increasingly a feature in my writings on art.

This article originally appeared in *The Post Modern Times.*

Further reading:

Michael Paraskos, *Clive Head* (Aldershot: Lund Humphries, 2010)
Michael Paraskos, *Regeneration* (Mitcham: Orage Press, 2010)
Clive Head, *Sun Setting Over Victoria* (Mitcham, Orage Press, 2012)
Clive Head, *From Victoria to Arcadia* (London: Marlborough Fine Art, 2012)
Pierluigi Sacco, 'Money for Nothing' in *Flash Art Italia,* no. 303, June 2012 (in Italian)

The Aphorisms of Irsee

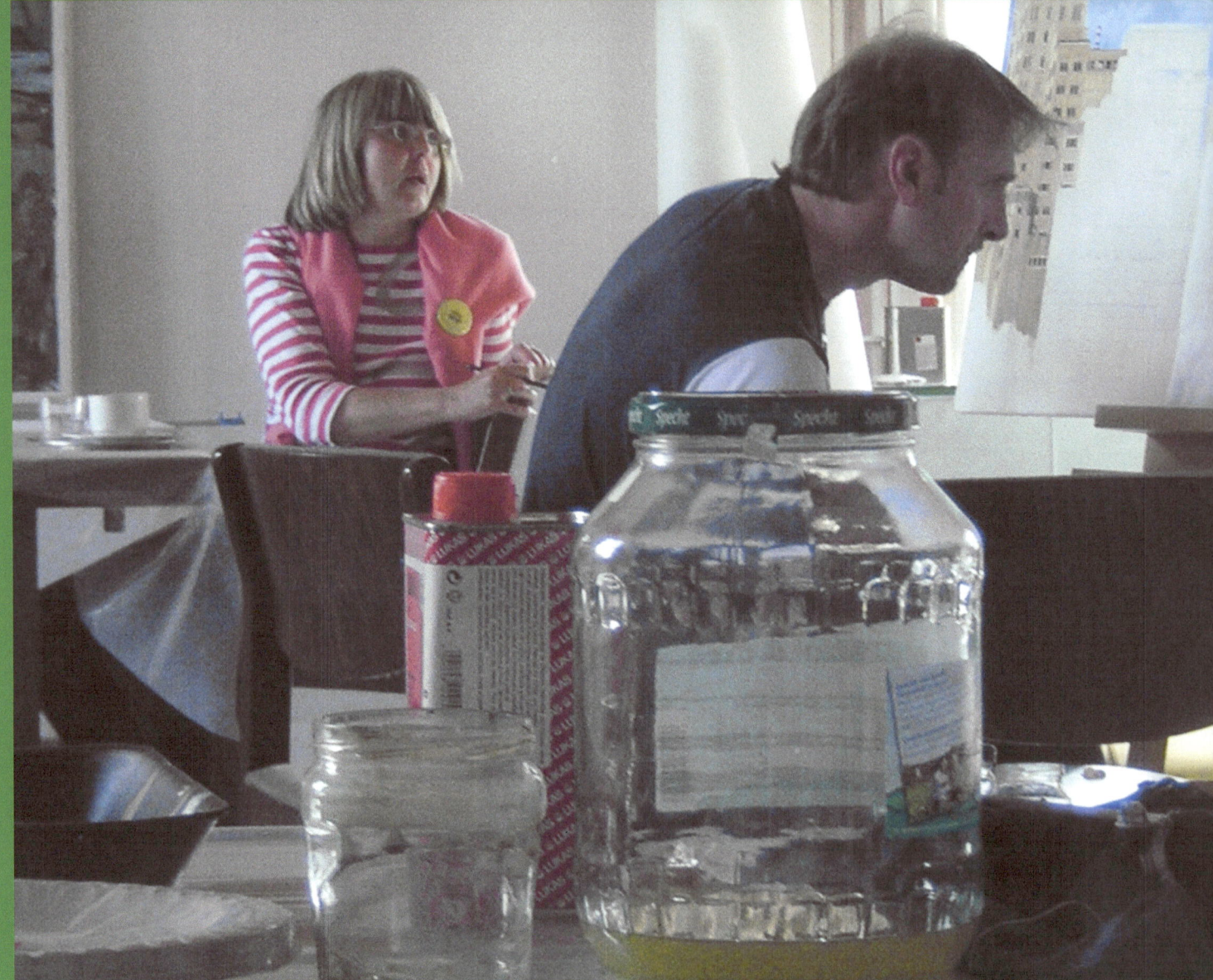

1. Art is always definitive, but never dogmatic.
2. Artists should slow down and experience the world. A quiet cup of coffee is often the best starting point for art.

3. All artists create heavens. The heaven of God; or, the anti-heaven of the Devil; or, the earthly heaven of humankind.
4. Photography kills painting when the painter merely copies a photograph. It turns the artist into a photocopying machine.
5. Reproduction is never enough. Art is always a creative act.
6. To illustrate ideas is merely to repeat those ideas and turns artists into parrots.
7. The artist creates form, and through form creates reality.
8. In the artwork politics is always subservient to art. Art does not illustrate politics.
9. The primary purpose of art is the establishment and organisation of believable space.
10. Art is the organisation of space, but the creation of mundane space is a worthless exercise.
11. True art comes from an aesthetic engagement with the world by a particular person, in a particular place, at a particular time.
12. The artist creates form and space through a direct engagement with the world, a physical engagement with their materials, and a personal engagement with their own sense of self. That is what aesthetics means in art.
13. Through art we can confront suffering, but only if our aim is to to alleviate pain, rather than wallow in it.
14. Even great art that shows suffering is a refuge from pain. It is balm for the human spirit.
15. Art should astonish its viewer, but most art is too mean-spirited to do this.

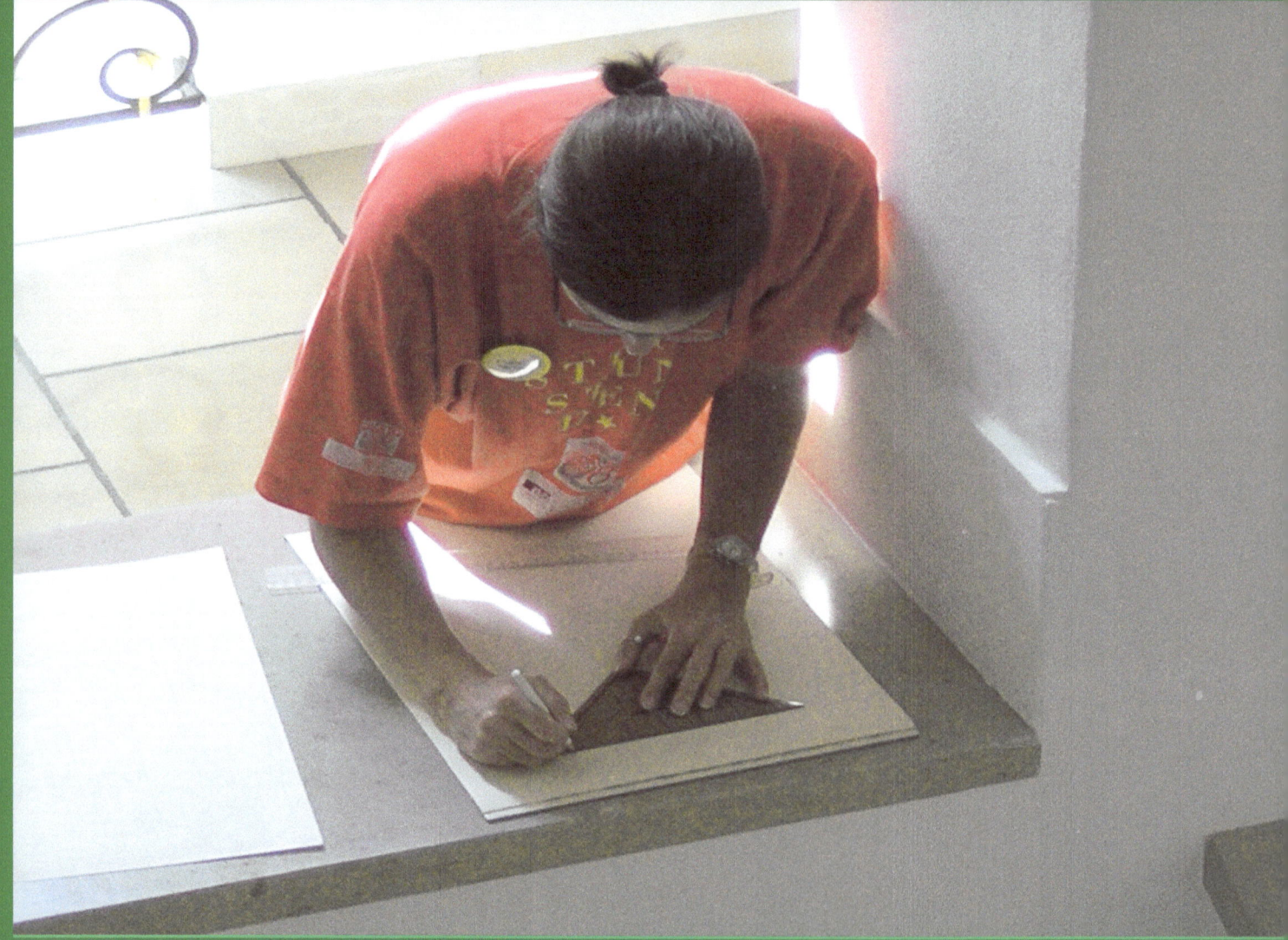

16. No idea in art is better than any other idea. This means an artwork dealing with torture, murder or any other form of inhumanity is not automatically better than an artwork that deals with a still life or gentle landscape. It is a harsh truth, but death and the teapot really are of equal value in art.

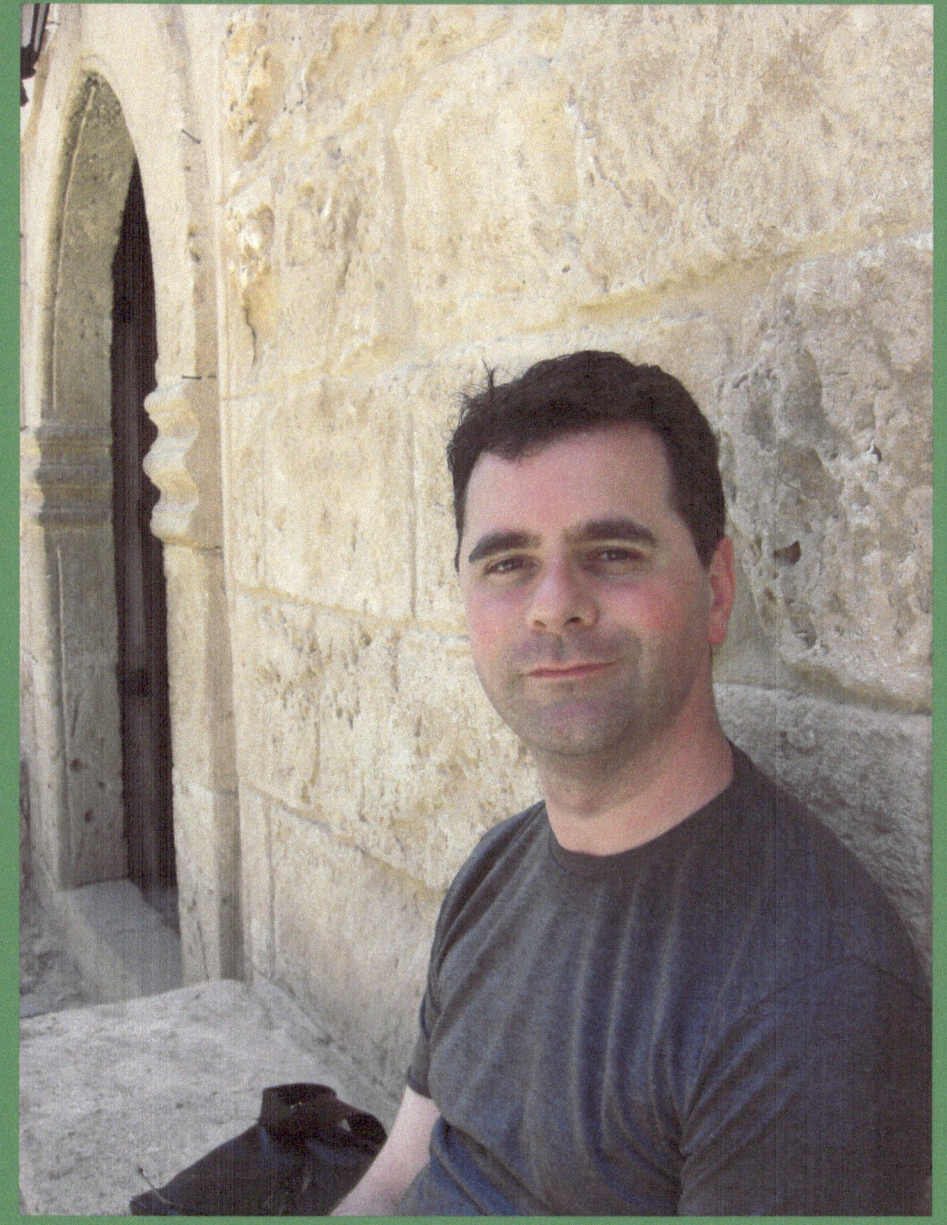

17. Art does not need to be religious, but it is always quasi-religious.
18. Faith in art requires faith in the validity of art.
19. The dominance of conceptual illustration shows bad faith in art.

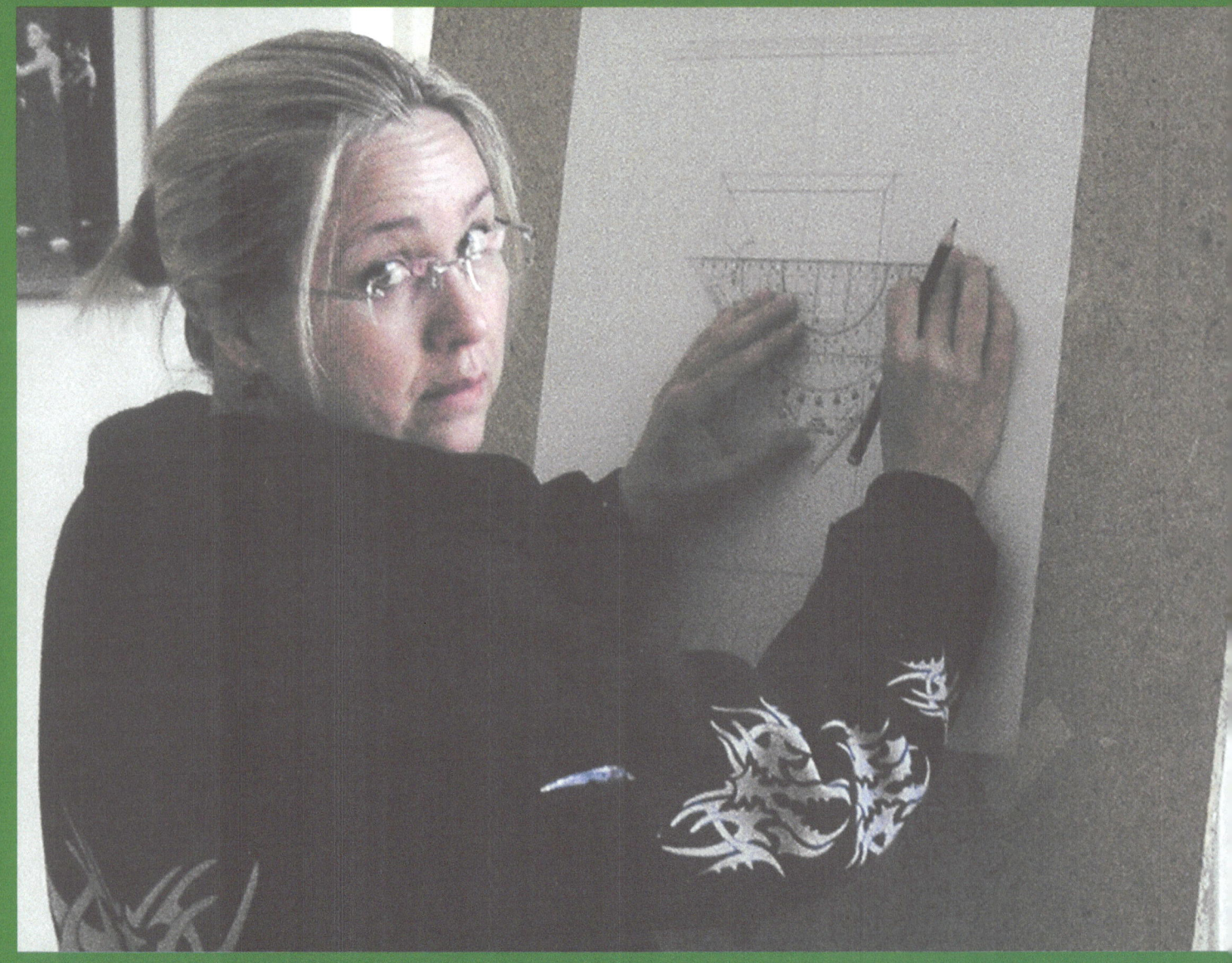

20. Art is never ironic. It can be funny, witty or playful, but the artist always means it.

21. Art is not literature, art is not politics, art is not philosophy. So why is art polluted by the discourses of literature, politics and philosophy? Why is art a polluted framework?
22. Art is always a sensuous act. It is the expression of the aesthetic experience of existence. Aesthetics in art means 'the sensuous'.
23. For artists aesthetics is always materialistic and art always an object.
24. Art has a nationality: the German artist cannot make English art because they are German. They can only make German art.
25. Art has a nationality: the English artist cannot make German art because they are English. They can only make English art.
26. The lack of a history of making art stunts the progress of art.
27. Art without roots is like a tree without roots: dead.
28. Art is always formed by the individual sensibility of the artist, but it must transcend this if the artwork is to deserve another viewer.
29. The artist has to persuade the viewer that the reality they show is true.
30. Art is expression, not a cliché of expression.
31. Art is always political, but nothing kills the political power of art more effectively than political art.
32. The only mandate of the artist is to make art.
33. The power of art is not the power of the fist or the shriek of the sloganeer. Art quietly conquers receptive minds.
34. Scholarship is the enemy of romance. All art is romantic.

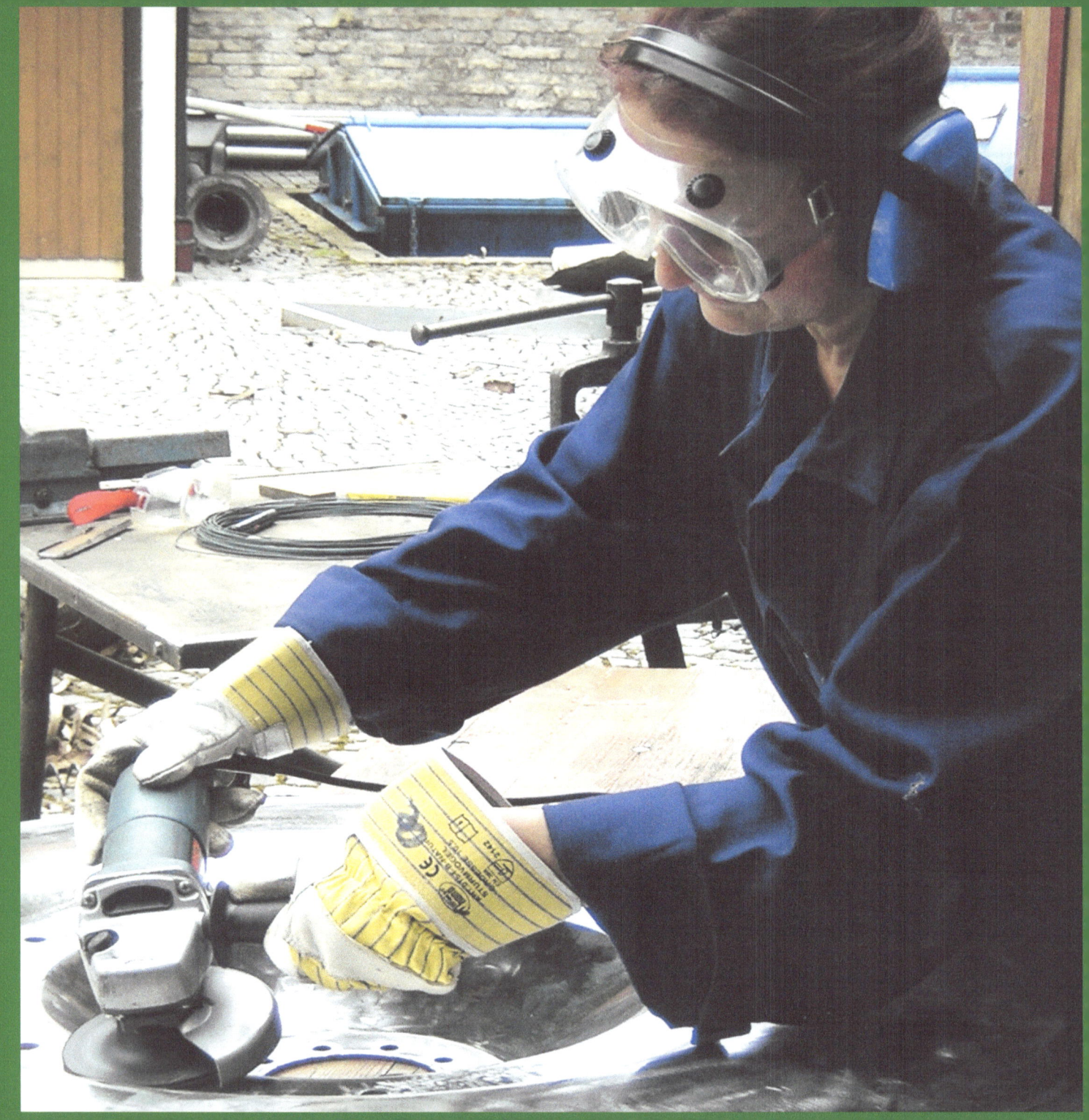

35. Chaos is not the absence of order, it is order beyond human comprehension. That is why it is so terrifying.
36. Chaos provokes fear *(Grundangst)*. Art orders chaos.
37. True art fixes the flux of chaos. That is how we cope with chaos, and that is the purpose of art.
38. Performance is not art: it moves too much and so adds to the flux. Art is always a moment of longed-for stasis.
39. All painting presents a barrier to the viewer. It is called the picture plane. To overcome this both the artist and viewer must perform acts of transubstantiation.
40. Non-art is never transformative and so should never be called art, even if it is made of paint.
41. To call art a language shows the paucity of the language with which we discuss art.
42. Most art schools do not teach art. They do not teach anything.
43. The framework of art is not a free-for-all. It is as specific as physics to the physicist, brain surgery to the surgeon, or plumbing to the plumber.
44. The scandal of the art world is not that so much rubbish is called art, but that so little of the good stuff is.
45. Art can be made from anything, but not everything can be art.
46. Some things are not art.
47. One should choose whether to make tables or bake cakes, and not be a carpenter of cakes or a baker of tables.

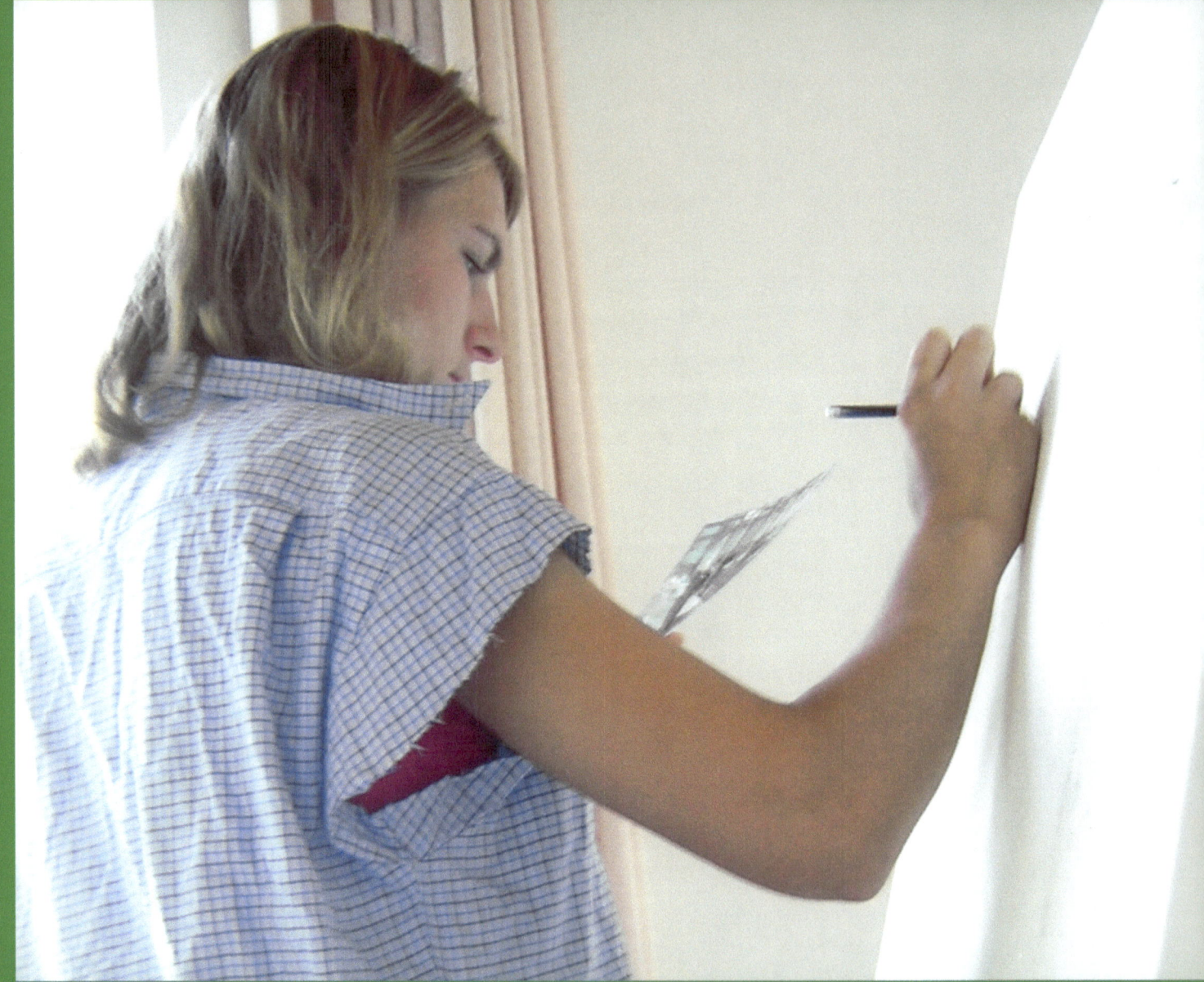

48. Communion is not the salvation of one, but the salvation of all.
    Art is also not the salvation of one, but must be for all.
49. Those who preach loudest often have least to say.

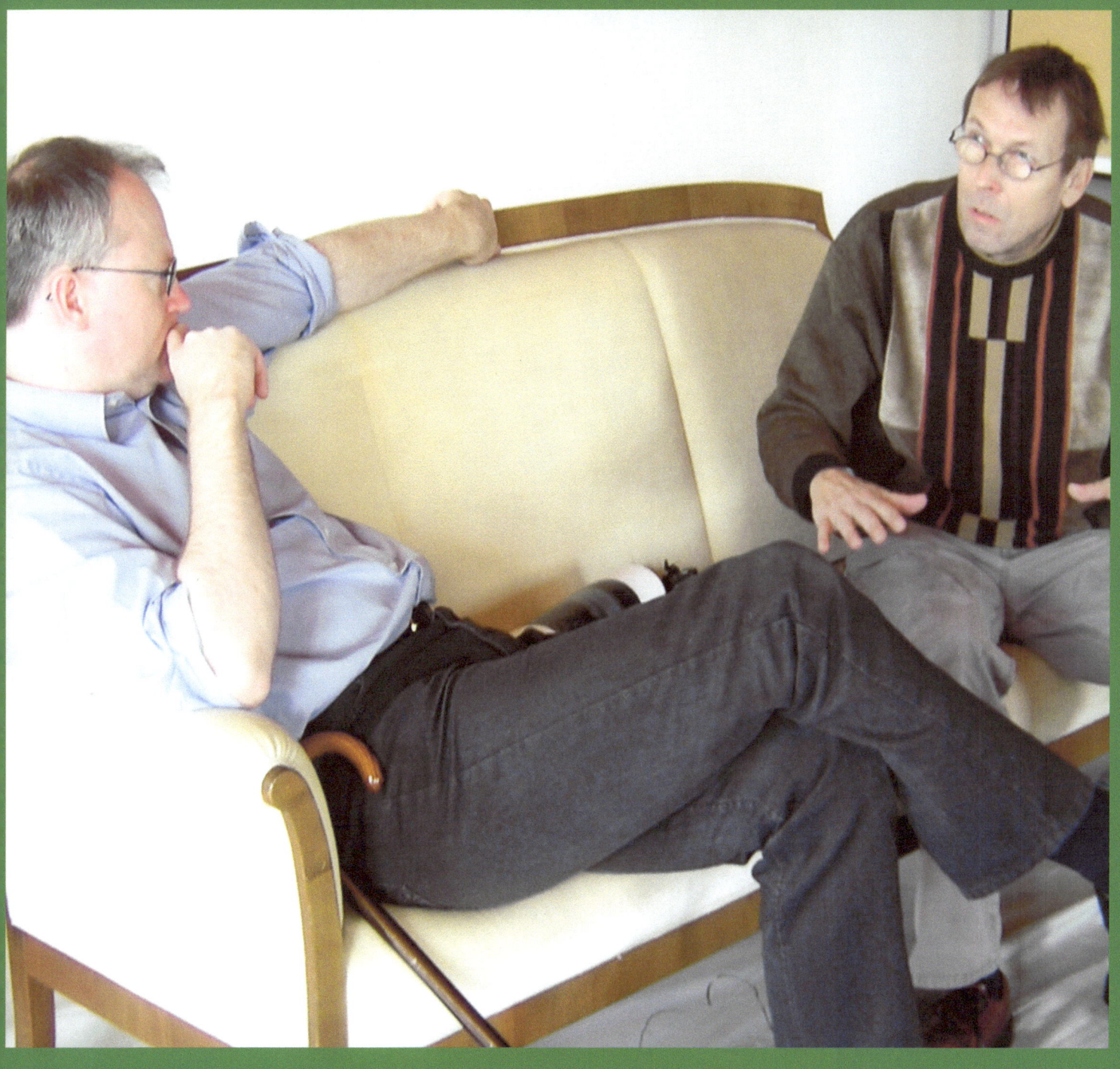

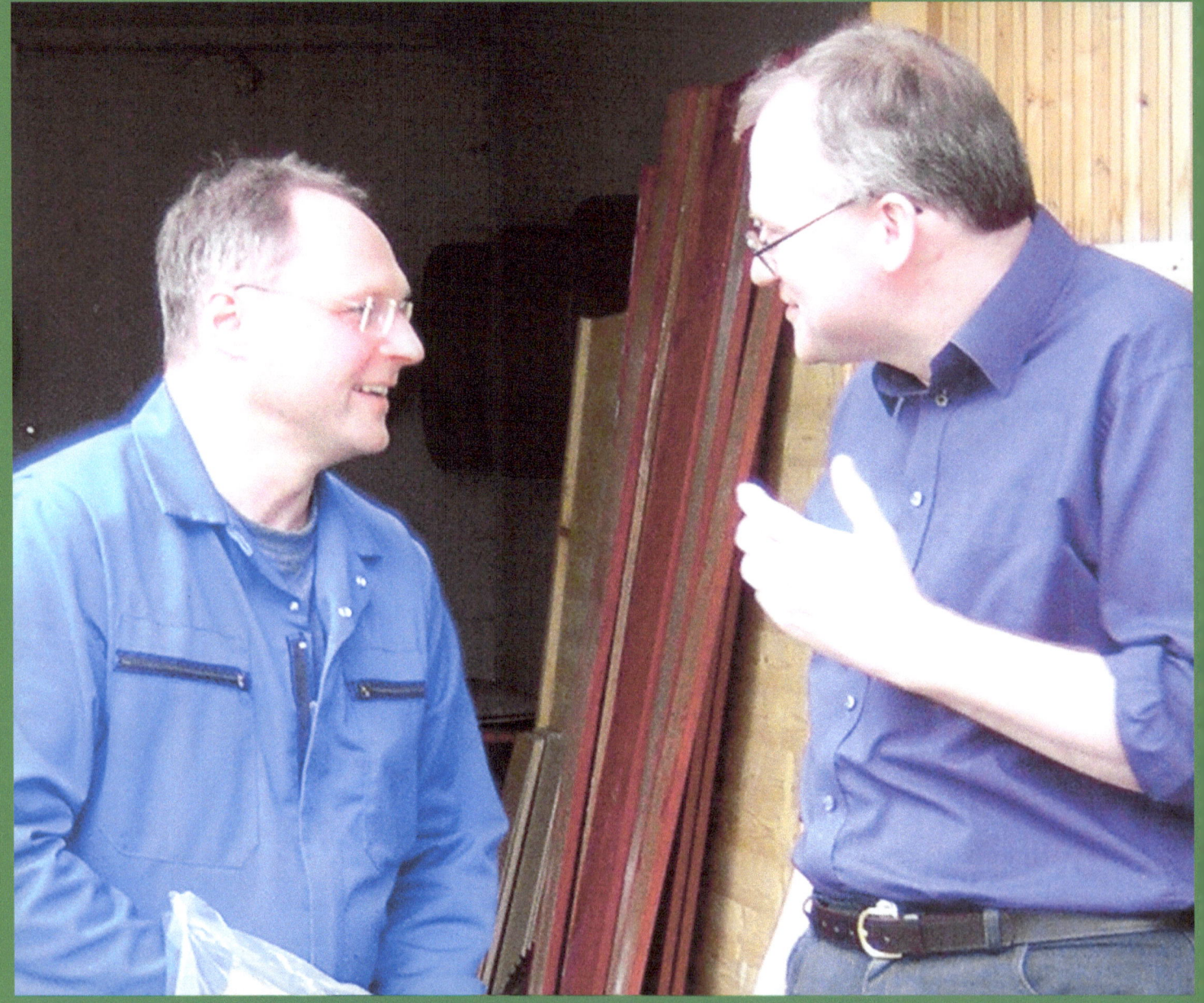

50. Art doesn't require us to wash our dirty linen in public.
51. Sometimes even the artist should realise it is too cold to go for
    a swim.

52. One should live for one's art, but there is no need to die for it.
53. The realist artist and the abstract artist speak the same language, the language of art. The real divide is between True Art and non-art.
54. Conceptualism might be important, significant and necessary, but that does not make it art.
55. Bad art demeans nature and, because of this, bad art is immoral.
56. Should artists practice what they preach?
57. Ich möchte ein bier bitte.
58. Tolerance is best learnt by example, not by reminders of guilt.
59. Three artists make a movement. Four make an art school.
60. You do not need electricity to make art.
61. Central heating has destroyed English art. It has removed the artist from feeling the real world.
62. You can spot a Berlin artist at a hundred paces. Two hundred if they're talking.
63. In Germany there are some things we cannot say.
64. In England there are some things we cannot say.
65. Why have there been no great painters since 1945?
66. Ruskin said no work of art should ever be perfect. For most artists this is not an issue.
67. It looks like art, but looks can deceive us.
68. A few years study at university is only the start. You should add another ten years hard work to deserve the name of artist.

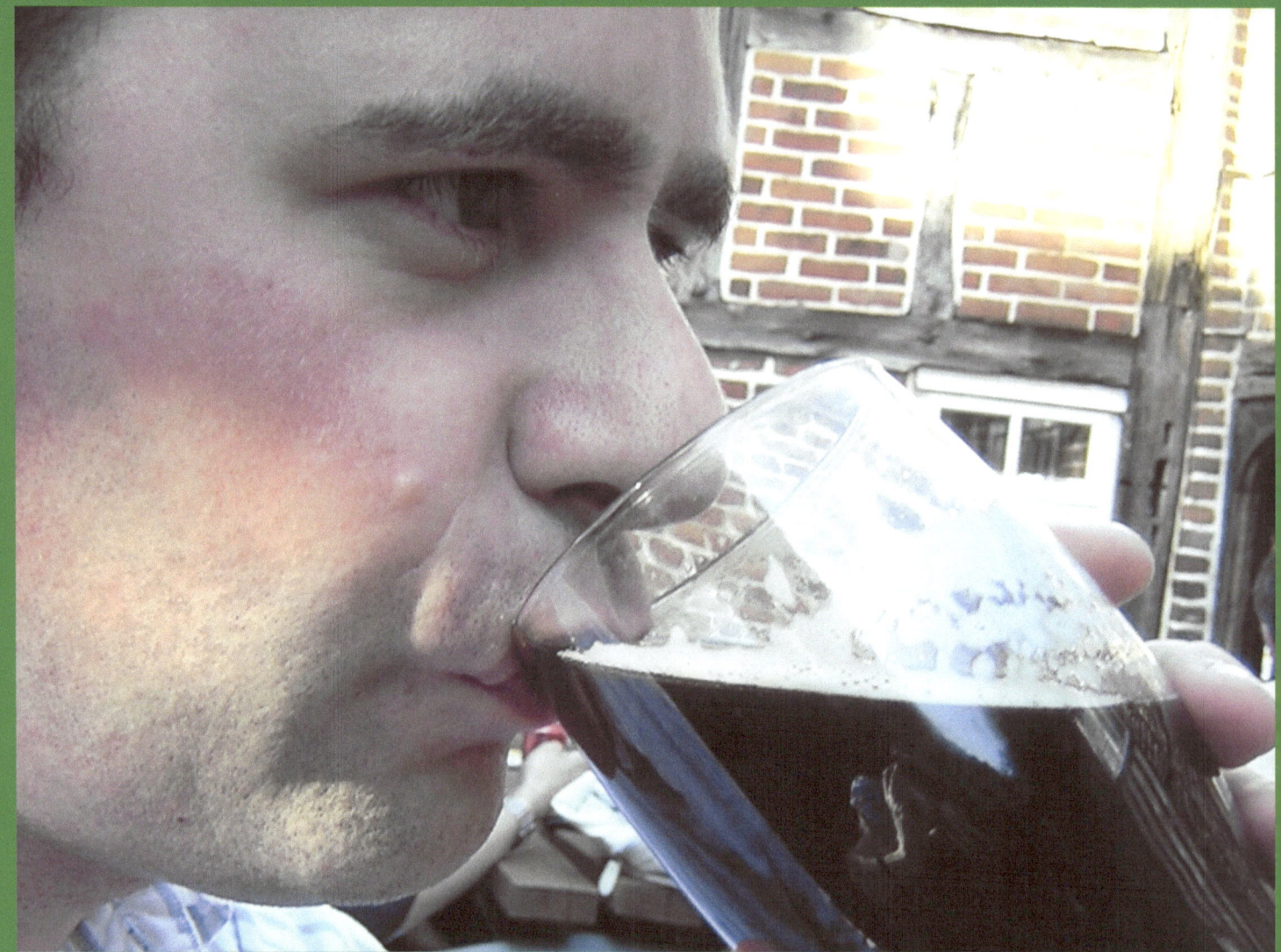

69. Drawing too much attention to the materiality of a painting
    turns it into sculpture.
70. The framework of painting and the framework of sculpture
    might overlap, but they are not the same.
71. Photography is too insistent on its own material nature ever to be
    art. It cannot not be itself.

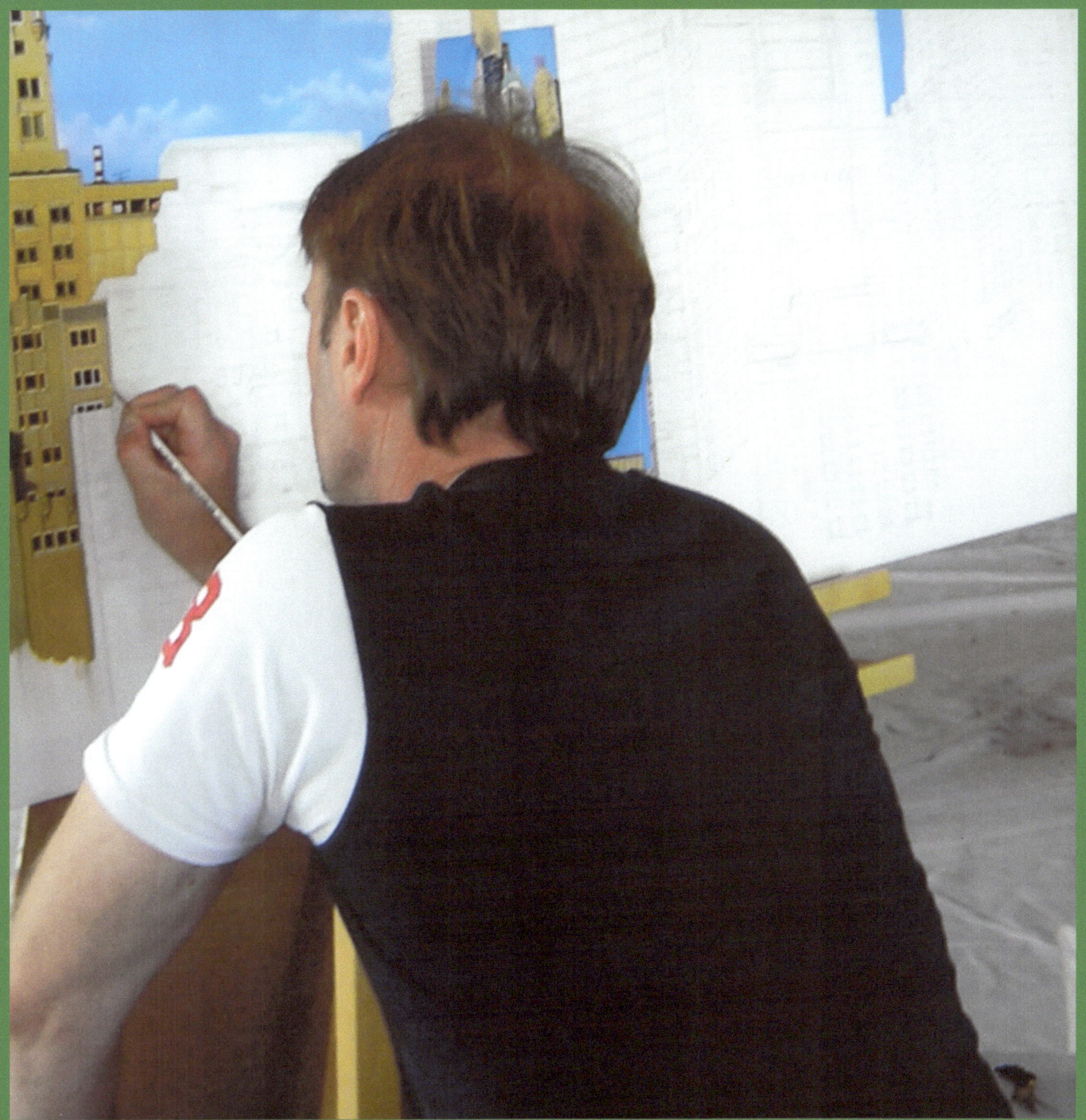

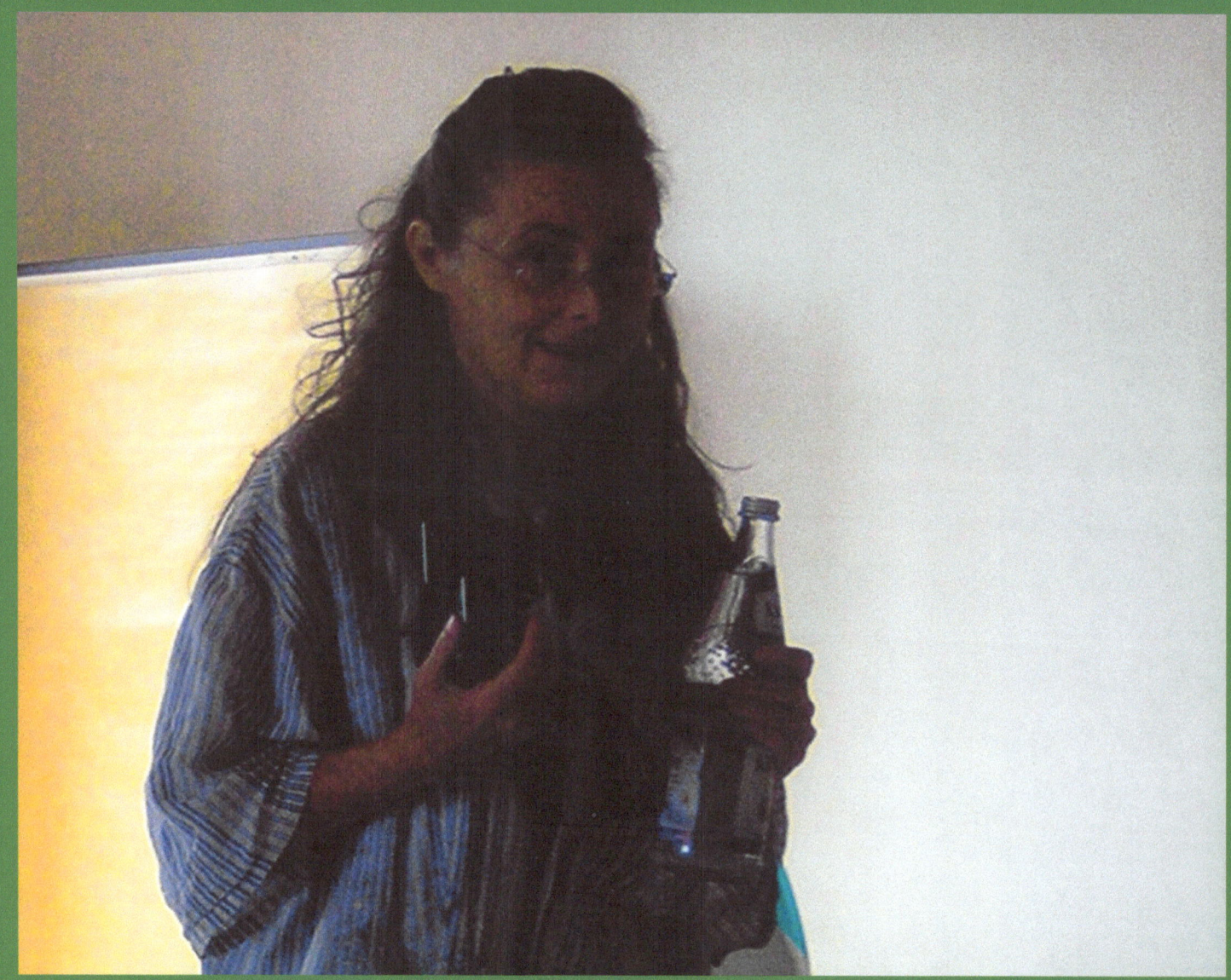

72. The most serious statements can come from laughter.
73. Humour can hide anger.
74. Idealism is lost on the young.
75. Beware the Swiss bearing sausages.

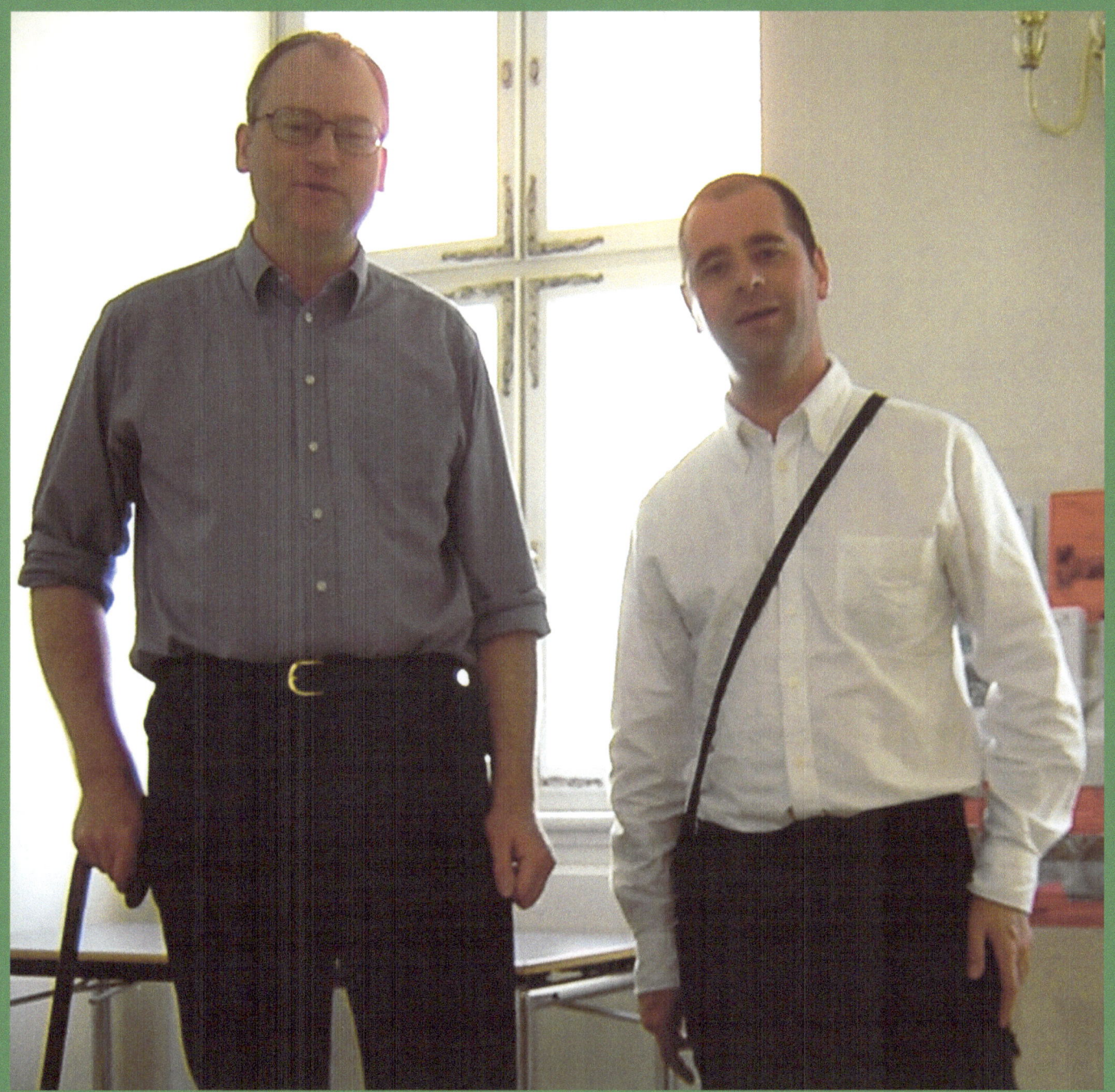

www.ingramcontent.com/pod-product-compliance
Lightning Source LLC
Chambersburg PA
CBHW050436180526
45159CB00006B/2563